THE USBORNE PICTURE DICTIONARY

Angela Wilkes
Illustrated by Colin King

Consultant: Betty Root

Fifi   Zizi   Sam Strongman   The dogs   Pop

Aa

about

This book is about dragons.

above

The kite is above the tree.

accident

Henry has an accident.

actor

This is a famous actor.

add

Aggie adds sugar to her tea.

address

This is Henry's address.

aeroplane

This aeroplane is green.

afraid

The dog is afraid of mice.

after

Tuesday comes after Monday. It follows Monday. It does not come before it.

It is after midnight. It is later than midnight.

Ben reads after dinner. He reads when dinner is finished.

afternoon

The afternoon is the part of the day that comes after midday and before evening.

Tim plays football on Saturday afternoon.

Come and spend the afternoon with me.

again

Henry has an accident again.

against

Fifi is leaning against a wall.

age

These men are the same age. They are both 70 years old.

air

The aeroplane is in the air.

airport

The pilot can see the airport.

alarm clock

The alarm clock is ringing. It wakes up Henry.

all

All the mice are pink.

almost

Pop has almost finished the puzzle.

alone

Fifi is all alone. No one is with her.

along

Flowers grow along the path.

alphabet

All these letters are in the alphabet.

already

Zizi already has a cake.

also

Bill is a man. Ben is also a man. He is a man too.

Give me an apple and also two bananas.

Fifi is not only beautiful, she is also clever.

always

Henry always has accidents.

ambulance

The ambulance is coming to take Henry to hospital.

among

The cat is among the birds.

and

Here are Fritz and Hank.

angel

The angel is flying.

angry

The angel is angry.

animal

These are all animals.

another

Bill takes another cake.

answer

Here is a sum and its answer.
Is the answer right?

ant

The ant is running across the book.

any

Have you any eggs?
Have you some eggs?

You can buy a newspaper at any newsagent's (at no matter which newsagent's).

anybody

Is anybody there?
Is somebody there?

apple

Fifi is eating an apple.

apron

Bill is wearing an apron.

argue

Bill and Ben are arguing.

arm

Ben has a broken arm.

armchair

The cat is asleep in an armchair.

army

Bill is in the army.

arrange

Fifi is arranging the flowers.

arrive

The train is arriving.

arrow

Holmes has found an arrow.

artist

The artist is painting.

as

It was raining as we left. It was raining then.

As it is raining, he is staying at home. He is staying at home because it is raining.

Bill is as tall as Ben.

ask

Zizi asks for an apple.

astronaut

Here is an astronaut.

at

The children are at school, Bill is at home and Ben is at work.

At seven o'clock Henry gets up.

Ben is good at French.

aunt

Aunt Aggie is Mum's sister.

B b

baby

The baby is crying.

back

Henry is scratching his back.

bad

Sam is a bad boy. He is not good.

The weather is bad today.

Father is in a bad mood.

She has a bad cold.

badge

Bill has a lot of badges.

bag

The bag is full of money.

baker

The baker is making bread.

ball

Max catches the ball.

balloon

Zizi is chasing a balloon.

banana

A big bunch of bananas.

band

The band is playing music.

bank

Jim is on the river bank.

bank

Fred is running away from the bank.

bark

The dog is barking.

basket

The basket is full of apples.

bath

The cat is in the bath.

bathroom

The bath is in the bathroom.

beach

Fifi is lying on the beach.

beak

The bird has a red beak.

bean

These are green beans.

bear

Bruno is a brown bear.

beard

The man has a long beard.

beautiful

A beautiful princess.

because

The baby is crying because she is hungry. That is the reason she is crying.

He is fat because he eats too much.

We must run because we are late.

bed

The king is in bed.

bedroom

The bed is in the bedroom.

bee

The bee is on a flower.

beef

Bill is carving the beef.
Beef is meat from cows.

beer

Bill is drinking beer.

before

Monday comes before
Tuesday. It does not come
after it.

It is before midnight. It is
earlier than midnight.

Why didn't you tell me before?
(earlier).

begin

It is beginning to rain.
It is starting to rain.

The film begins at 7 o'clock
and ends at 9 o'clock.

I am beginning school soon.

behind

Who is behind the tree?

believe

Sam believes in ghosts. He
thinks they really exist.

Sam believes anything you tell
him. He thinks everything you
tell him is true.

Pop believes in God.

bell

The bell is ringing.

belong

That bicycle belongs to me. It
is mine.

The hat belongs to Ben. It is
Ben's hat.

Ben belongs to a club. He is a
member of it.

below

The cat is below Bruno.
Bruno is above the cat.

belt

Fifi is wearing a big belt.

bench

The bird is on a bench.

bend

Sam is bending a spoon.

best

Fifi is the best dancer. She is a
better dancer than anyone
else.

Do your best:
Try as hard as you can.

Who is your best friend?

better

Fifi is a better dancer than Susie. Susie is a good dancer but Fifi is a very good dancer.

Henry speaks French better than Ben.

I was ill yesterday but I feel better now.

between

The cat is sitting between the two bears.

bicycle

The baker is riding a bicycle.

big

The elephant is big.

bird

The bird is on a bicycle.

birthday

It is Zizi's birthday today.

bite

The dog is biting the postman.

black

The big cat is black.

blackbird

A blackbird is black.

blackboard

Ben is writing on the blackboard.

blanket

There is a red blanket on the bed.

blind

A dog is leading the blind man.

blood

Sam has blood on his finger.

blow

Zizi is blowing out the candles.

blue

The house is blue.

boat

Three men in a boat.

body

Sam has a strong body.

bone

Fluff has a big bone.

bonfire

The bonfire is burning.

book

The book is about boats.

bookshop

Bill looks in the bookshop.

boot

The bird is wearing a blue boot.

both

Both of the pigs are pink.

bottle

A big bottle of wine.

bottom

The frog is at the bottom of the ladder.

bowl

The bowl is full of bananas.

box

The cat is asleep in a box.

boy

Tom is a little boy.

bracelet

Zizi is wearing a blue bracelet.

branch

The bird is standing on the branch of a tree.

bread

Bill is cutting the bread.

break

Ben breaks the bread in half.

breakfast

Fifi has her breakfast.

breathe

Fish can breathe underwater.

brick

The builder is carrying a brick.

bride

A beautiful bride . . .

bridegroom

. . . and her bridegroom.

bridge

Bill crosses the bridge.

bright

The star is bright.

bring

Max brings Bill a slipper.

brother

Bill and Ben are brothers.

brown

Bruno is a brown bear.

brush

Fritz is brushing his shoes.

bubble

Bruno is blowing a bubble.

bucket

Bill empties the bucket.

bud

The plant has one bud.

build

The builder is building a house.

building

A house is a building.

bulb

The caterpillar is looking at the flower bulb.

bull

The angry bull is chasing Bill.

bulldozer

Ben drives a bulldozer.

bump

Henry has hit a bump.

bunch

A big bunch of flowers.

burglar

The burglar runs away.

burn

The house is burning!

bus

The bus is stopping.

bus stop

Fifi is waiting at the bus stop.

bush

Who is behind the bush?

busy

The man is busy. He has a lot of work to do.

but

Bill eats a lot, but he is not fat.

I like sweets, but I do not like chocolate.

I want a new dress, but I have no money.

butcher

The butcher sells meat.

butter

The butter is melting.

butterfly

The butterfly is sitting on a flower.

button

Fifi is sewing on a button.

buy

Fifi buys some bananas. She pays money for them.

by

The man is standing by the car.

cabbage

Fifi chooses a cabbage.

café

The friends are going to a café.

cage

The lion is in a cage.

cake

Fifi is cutting the cake.

calculator

The man is using his calculator.

calendar

Aggie is looking at the calendar.

calf

The calf is with its mother.

call

The farmer calls the calf. He shouts to it to come to him.

camel

Henry is riding a camel.

camera

Bill has a new camera.

camp

Bill and Ben are camping.

candle

Henry is carrying a candle.

cap

Fred is wearing a cap.

capital

Rome is the capital of Italy. It is the main city.

Paris is the capital of France.

'A' is a capital letter and 'a' is a small letter.

car

Fred has a fast car.

caravan

He also has a caravan.

card

The men are playing a game of cards.

cardigan

Aggie is wearing a pink cardigan.

carpet

The carpet is blue.

carrot

The man is holding a bunch of carrots.

carry

Zizi is carrying the carrots.

castle

The castle is on a hill.

cat

The cat is asleep on the carpet.

catch

The cat is catching a ball.

caterpillar

The caterpillar is eating a leaf.

cauliflower

A cauliflower in a basket.

cave

There is treasure in the cave.

ceiling

Sam can reach the ceiling.

cellar

The cellar is full of wine.

chain

The watch is on a chain.

chair

Bruno is sitting on a chair.

chalk

Bruno is writing with chalk on a blackboard.

change

Bill is counting his change.

change

Henry is changing a wheel.

chase

Henry is chasing a thief.

cheap

The chair is cheap. It does not cost much.

cheek

Nan has pink cheeks.

cheese

Fifi is eating cheese.

chemist's

Henry buys pills at the chemist's.

cheque

Bill writes a cheque to pay for what he buys.

cherry

The bird is eating the cherries.

chest

Sam is beating his chest.

chick

The hen has five chicks.

chicken

Ben is cutting the chicken.

child, children

The children are playing.

chimney

The bird is sitting on a chimney.

chimpanzee

The chimpanzee is swinging from a tree.

chin

Sam is rubbing his chin.

chips

Ben has a plate of chips.

chocolate

Zizi is eating chocolate.

choose

Fifi chooses a red dress. She picks it out.

chop

Ben has a chop for dinner.

Christmas

It is Christmas. Father Christmas is here.

church

Fifi is going to church.

cigarette

The man is smoking a cigarette.

cinema

Fifi is at the cinema. She is watching a film.

circle

Ten chicks are walking in a circle.

circus

A clown at the circus.

city

A city is a very big town. Many people live there.

class

There are five children in the class.

classroom

The classroom is empty.

clean

Bill puts on a clean apron. The other one is dirty.

clean

Henry is cleaning his car.

clever

Brains is clever. He learns fast.

cliff

Henry is standing on a cliff.

climb

Sam is climbing the cliff.

clock

Ben is cleaning the clock.

close

Fifi closes the window.

cloud

The angel is lying on a cloud.

clown

A clown from the circus.

coach

The coach is full of clowns.

coast

Trees grow along the coast.
The coast is by the sea.

coat

The king has a big coat.

cobweb

A spider makes a cobweb.

cockerel

The cockerel is calling.

coffee

Fifi pours the coffee.

coin

Fifi puts coins in her purse.

cold

Oscar is cold. He is not warm.

colour

There are seven colours in the rainbow.

comb

Fifi has a big comb.

comb

Fifi combs her hair with her comb.

come

The duck is coming towards Zizi.

comic

The boys are reading a comic.

computer

Brains is working on a computer.

conductor

Herbert is a conductor. He conducts an orchestra.

cook

Henry is cooking dinner.

cooker

His cooker is very old.

cork

The cork pops out of the bottle.

corn

Corn is growing in the field.

corner

Ruff is in a corner.

cost

The ring costs £1000. You must pay £1000 for it.

cotton

Fifi is sewing with cotton thread.

cough

Fifi is coughing.

count

Zizi is counting the cakes to see how many there are.

country

England is a small country.

China and India are big countries.

How many countries are there in the world?

country

Dan lives in the country, not in a town.

cover

Bill covers his head with a newspaper.

cow

The cow has a friend on its back.

cowboy

The cowboy is chasing the cow.

crab

A crab runs sideways.

crane

The crane is lifting the car.

crayon

Zizi draws with crayons.

cream

There is cream on the cake.

crocodile

The crocodile is asleep.

cross

Three mice on a red cross.

cross

Henry is crossing the road.

crossroads

He stops at the crossroads.

crown

The king wears a crown.

cry

The king is crying.

cube

A cube has six sides.

cucumber

The mice are carrying a cucumber.

cup

A caterpillar is looking in the cup.

cupboard

The cup is in the cupboard.

curtain

Fifi opens the curtains.

cushion

The crown is on a cushion.

customer

The customer is buying bread from the baker.

cut

Fifi is cutting Ben's hair.

cut out

Fifi is cutting out a picture.

dance

Fifi is dancing with Sam.

dancer

She wants to be a dancer.

danger

Henry is in danger. He is not safe.

dare

The man does not dare dive. He is afraid to dive.

dark

The room is dark. It is not light.

daughter

Zizi is Mary's daughter. Mary is Zizi's mother.

day

There are 365 days in a year.

There are seven days in a week: Sunday, Monday, Tuesday, Wednesday, Thursday, Friday and Saturday.

There are 24 hours in a day.

dead

Max is pretending to be dead but he is really alive.

decide

Bill decides to buy a car. He makes up his mind to buy one.

Decide which dress you want. Make up your mind which one you want.

Decide what you want to do.

deep

Fifi is in deep water.

deer

A deer meets Max.

dentist

The dentist is looking at Henry's teeth.

describe

Bill describes the thief to the police.
He tells them what the thief looks like.

Can you describe the picture?

Can you say what it looks like?

desert

Camels live in the desert.

desk

Jake is working at his desk.

diamond

Fred has found a diamond.

dictionary

Fritz has a dictionary. It is a book of words.

die

Henry's plant is dying. Soon it will be dead.

different

The men are wearing different hats.'

dig

Max is digging a hole.

dining room

The mice are eating in the dining room.

dinner

A monster is eating his dinner.

dinosaur

The dinosaur is eating his dinner.

direction

Max is changing direction to go the other way.

dirty

The dinosaur is dirty.

dish

A dish full of strawberries.

do

Henry is doing nothing.

doctor

The doctor is examining Sam to see if he is ill.

dog

The dog is chasing a rabbit.

doll

Zizi is playing with a doll.

donkey

Henry is riding a donkey.

door

Fifi shuts the door.

downstairs

The doll is downstairs.

dragon

The dragon is breathing fire.

draw

Fifi is drawing a dragon.

drawing

This is her drawing.

dream

Henry dreams about spiders when he is asleep.

dress

Fifi is wearing a long dress.

dress

Fifi is dressing Zizi. She is putting on her clothes.

24

drink

Sam is drinking milk.

drive

Henry is driving his car to work.

drop

Henry drops an egg.

drum

Fred is playing his drum.

dry

The ground is very dry because it has not rained.

duck

The duck is in the bath.

dust

Max is rolling in the dust.

dustbin

Bill looks in the dustbin.

duvet

Fifi has a pink duvet on her bed.

each

Each child has a cake.

eagle

The eagle is on its nest.

ear

The donkey has long ears.

early

Ben gets up early in the morning. He does not get up late.

I am coming home early. I am coming home sooner than I usually do.

The shops close early on Monday.

earth

The earth is round.

east

The bird is facing east. East is opposite west.

Easter

Easter is a religious holiday in the Spring.
People do not go to work on Good Friday or Easter Monday.

easy

It is easy to make the cake. It is not difficult.

Sam's homework is easy.

I can easily finish my work in an hour.

eat

Zizi is eating chocolate.

edge

Zizi is sitting on the edge of the table.

egg

Zizi is eating an egg for breakfast.

elbow

Henry hits his elbow.

elephant

The elephant throws the man off its back.

empty

The bag is empty. There is nothing in it.

empty

Henry is emptying the bucket.

end

The mouse is swinging at the end of the rope.

enough

Fifi has enough money to buy a new car. She has as much money as she needs to buy it.

Have you had enough to eat? Have you had as much as you want?

enter

The king is entering the room.

entrance

Henry is standing at the entrance of the cave.

envelope

Fifi is opening the envelope.

escape

The prisoner escapes from the castle.

evening

The sun sets in the evening and it gets dark.

every

Every pig is pink. They are all the same colour.

everyone

Everyone is wearing a hat. Each person has one.

everything

Everything on the table is green.

everywhere

Fifi looks everywhere for her cat. She looks in every place.

My dog follows me everywhere.

except

Every pig is pink except for one.

exciting

Jake is reading an exciting book. It is a thriller.

exercise book

Tim is writing in his exercise book.

experiment

Brains does an experiment to see what will happen.

explain

Can you explain what happened?

Explain to me how it works.

Fifi explains why she wants a car. She makes it plain why she wants it.

eye

The cat has blue eyes.

face

Fifi is washing her face.

factory

This man works in a factory where cars are made.

fair

Fifi's friend has fair hair.

fairy

The fairy is sitting on a flower.

fall

The fairy falls off the flower.

family

A family of fairies.

famous

Will is a famous artist. He is well known.

far

The house is far away. It is not near.

farm

The farm is in the country.

farmer

The farmer lives in the farmhouse.

fast

The farmer runs fast.

fat

This fairy is fat. She eats too much.

father

Zizi is with her father. She is his daughter.

feather

The bird has yellow feathers.

feed

Zizi is feeding the ducks.

feel

Bill can feel the chair. He is touching it.

feet

Here are two big feet.

fence

The cow is jumping over the fence.

few

This bird has few feathers. He does not have many.

field

The cows are in a field.

fight

Bill and Ben are fighting.

fill

Fifi fills the glass with milk.

film

Fifi and Sam watch a film.

find

Ben finds the book he was looking for.

finger

A hand has four fingers and a thumb.

finish

Fifi finishes her dinner. She eats all of it.

fire

The men are sitting by the fire to keep them warm.

fireman

The firemen put out the fire.

fireworks

Fireworks in the sky.

first

Bill is first in the queue. Who is last?

fish

A fat fish meets a little fish.

fish

Tim is fishing. He wants to catch fish.

29

flag

Henry is carrying a flag.

flame

Zizi blows out the flame.

flat

This house has a flat roof.

flat

Fifi lives in a flat. She does not have a garden.

floor

Ruff is lying on the floor.

flour

Bill uses flour to make a cake.

flow

The river flows into the sea.

flower

Henry gives Fifi a flower.

fly

There is a fly on the flower.

fly

The fly is flying away.

fog

Henry cannot see much in the fog. He is lost.

follow

Henry is following a dog.

food

Jake is eating the food.

football

Sam kicks the football into the air.

for

The present is for Ben.

forehead

Henry hits his forehead.

forest

Many trees grow in a forest.

forget

Bill always forgets my name. He does not remember it.

I have forgotten where he lives.

Do not forget to come!

fork

Ben is holding a fork.

fox

The fox is red.

freeze

When water freezes, it turns into ice.

The pond freezes over in winter.

Fifi freezes food in the freezer (a powerful fridge).

fridge

Ben puts milk in the fridge to keep it cold.

friend

Sam and Fifi are friends. They like each other.

frighten

Fifi frightens her friend.

frog

The frog is jumping.

from

The letter is from France. It is from Pierre to Fifi.

Fritz comes from Germany.

I live ten miles from London.

front

Ben is in front of Bill in the queue.

frost

There is frost on the window. It was cold last night.

fruit

These are all different kinds of fruit.

fry

Ben is frying an egg.

frying pan

Eggs frying in a frying pan.

full

The bath is full of water.

funny

The clown is funny. He makes people laugh.

fur

The rabbit has white fur. Its fur is soft.

game

The children are playing a game of blindman's bluff.

garage

The car is in the garage.

garden

Flowers grow in the garden.

gas

Henry lights the gas.

gate

The farmer shuts the gate.

get up

Ben gets up at 7 o'clock.

ghost

The ghost touches Henry.

giant

A giant is a very big man.

giraffe

The giraffe is eating leaves.

girl

The little girl is chasing the cat.

32

give

The girl gives Ben a flower.

glass

The glass is full of milk.

glasses

Henry is wearing glasses to help him read.

glove

Sam is wearing a pair of red gloves.

go

The children are going to school.

goat

The goat is biting Henry.

gold

Fifi has a gold chain.

good

Ben is a good baker. He makes good bread.

goose

The goose is chasing the goat.

grape

Here is a bunch of grapes.

grapefruit

Fifi is eating a grapefruit.

grass

Ruff is rolling on the grass.

green

The grass is green.

grey

The big cat is grey.

grocer

The grocer sells food.

ground

Zizi is sitting on the ground.

group

Here is a group of boys.

grow

Zizi is growing. She is getting taller.

guest

Fifi welcomes the guest. He is coming to dinner.

guitar

Manuel is playing the guitar.

gun

Sam is firing the gun.

hair

Nan has white hair.

hairbrush

She brushes her hair with a pink hairbrush.

hairdresser

The hairdresser is cutting Fifi's hair.

half

Zizi has one half of the orange. Fifi has the other half.

ham

Bill is cutting the ham.

hammer

Henry is using the hammer.

hand

Henry hits his hand with the hammer.

handbag

Fifi is emptying her handbag.

handkerchief

Fifi is waving her handkerchief.

handle

The handle of the cup breaks.

hang

Henry is hanging from a rope.

happen

Where did the accident happen? Where did it take place.

What happened to him?

How often does this happen?

happy

Bill is happy to see Ben. He is pleased to see him.

harbour

The boats are in the harbour.

hard

The mattress is hard. It is not soft.

hat

Fifi is wearing a pretty hat.

have

Bill and Ben have two cats. The cats belong to them.

hay

The farmer cuts grass to make hay.

head

There is a bird on Henry's head.

headlights

The car's headlights are shining on the burglar.

hear

Pop cannot hear well.

heart

The heart is the muscle which pumps blood round your body.

When you run, your heart beats faster.

I love you with all my heart.

heavy

The rock is heavy. It is not light.

hedge

Henry is cutting the hedge.

hedgehog

This is a hedgehog.

helicopter

The helicopter is flying.

help

Bill is helping Ben to lift the piano.

hen

The hen is eating seeds.

here

I am here. I am in this place.

Put the chair here, not there.

I live here, in this house.

Come here. Come to this place.

hide

The thief is hiding under the bed.

high

What a high mountain!

high

The bird is high in the sky.

hill

The house is on a hill.

hippopotamus

A muddy hippopotamus.

hit

Zizi is hitting Ruff.

hold

The witch is holding a broom. She has it in her hand.

hole

Ruff is digging a hole.

holiday

Bill is on holiday. He does not have to work.

homework

Tim is doing the homework his teacher has given him.

honey

Zizi is eating the honey. It is sweet.

hook

The hat is hanging on a hook.

horse

Henry is riding a horse.

hospital

Henry is in hospital.

hot

The soup is hot. It is not cold.

hotel

Fifi is going to a hotel for a holiday.

hour

There are 24 hours in a day.

There are 60 minutes in an hour.

Ben works eight hours a day.

It takes me half an hour to get home.

house

Fritz lives in a big house.

hovercraft

A hovercraft goes across the sea fast.

how

How are you?

How do you make a cake? In what way do you make it?

How do you say that in French?

hungry

Zizi is hungry. She wants something to eat.

hurry

Henry is hurrying. He is walking fast.

husband

Fritz is Heidi's husband. He is married to her.

hut

The workman is in the hut.

ice

The pond is covered in ice.

ice cream

Zizi is eating an ice cream.

idea

Henry has an idea for what to do on his birthday.
He has thought of something to do.

I have had a good idea! I have thought of something good.

if

If you ask him, he will tell you.
Ask him and he will tell you.

Fifi asks if Sam is at home. "Is Sam at home?" she asks.

I shall come if I can.

ill

Bill is ill. He does not feel well.

important

The Prime Minister is an important person. She has a lot of power.

It is important that you come. It matters a lot that you come.

in

The cat is in the basket.

insect

These are insects.

instead

Bill is going to the shop instead of Ben. Bill is going in place of Ben.

Fifi eats honey instead of sugar.

He is playing instead of working. He should be working.

invite

Fifi has invited 20 people to her party. She has asked 20 people to come.

She has sent everyone an invitation.

iron

This is an iron.

iron

Henry is ironing his shirt.

island

An island is surrounded by sea.

jacket

Fritz has a green jacket.

jam

A jar of strawberry jam.

jar

The jar is empty.

jeans

This is a pair of jeans.

jewels

The burglar can see the jewels on the table.

join

Bill is joining two wires together.

joke

Bill tells Ben a joke to make him laugh.

jug

Fifi is pouring the milk out of the jug.

jump

One frog is jumping over the other frog.

kangaroo

The kangaroo is jumping.

keep

Fifi wants to keep the dress she borrowed. She wants to have it for ever.

Can I keep what I have found?

It keeps raining. The rain does not stop.

kennel

Ruff sleeps in a kennel.

kettle

The kettle is boiling.

key

The key is hanging on a hook.

kick

Sam kicks the ball.

kill

The prince has killed the dragon. It is dead.

kind

Jim is kind to animals. He is gentle with them.

kind

An apple is a kind of fruit. It is a sort of fruit.

An onion is a kind of vegetable.

What kind of cake is it?

king

The king is wearing a crown.

kiss

Fifi is kissing Sam.

kitchen

Ben cooks in the kitchen.

kite

Bill is flying a kite.

kitten

A kitten is a baby cat.

knee

Henry falls on his knee.

knife

Bill cuts bread with a knife.

knit

Henry is knitting.

knitting

This is his knitting.

knock

Sam knocks at the door.

knot

There is a knot in the string.

know

Fritz knows how to swim. He can swim.

I know that two and two make four. I have learnt it.

Sam knows Ben. He has met him.

lace

The dress is made of lace.

ladder

Henry climbs the ladder.

lake

There are boats on the lake.

lamb

A lamb is a baby sheep.

lamp

Fifi is reading by the lamp.

last

Ben is the last in the queue. Who is first?

last

The film lasts an hour. It goes on for an hour.

The good weather lasted for five days.

How long will the rain last?

late

Tim is late for school. He is not on time.

He goes to bed late, not early.

It is too late to go for a walk.

laugh

Ben is laughing at Bill.

lawn

Fifi is mowing the lawn. The lawn is made of grass.

lazy

Tim is lazy. He does not like working.

lead

Ben is leading the children. He shows them the way.

lead

The dog is on a lead. It stops him running away.

leaf

The ant is carrying a leaf.

lean

Bruno is leaning on a fence.

learn

Fifi is learning how to drive. She is finding out how to drive.

You learn things at school.

I am learning French.

A teacher helps you to learn.

leather

This bag is made of leather. Leather is animal skin.

leave

Fifi is leaving the house. She is going away.

leek

The mice are carrying a leek.

left

Fritz is turning left.

leg

Henry is skating on one leg.

lemon

Fifi is cutting a lemon in half.

lesson

The class is having a lesson. They are learning.

letter

Sam is reading a letter.

lettuce

The caterpillar finds a lettuce.

library

Bill borrows books from the library.

lick

Zizi is licking her ice cream.

lid

Bill is putting the lid on the jar.

life

Butterflies have a short life. They do not live long.

He saved my life. He stopped me from dying.

I have known her all my life.

lift

Henry enters the lift to go to the top floor.

lift

The crane is lifting a car.

light

The dancer is light. She is not heavy.

light

A light is shining at the window.

light

Fritz lights a match.

lighthouse

The lighthouse is by the sea.

lightning

Lightning flashes in the sky.

like

Fifi likes Ben. He is her friend.

line

The five pigs are standing in a line.

lion

The lion is roaring.

lip

The clown has big red lips.

list

Henry is writing a long list.

listen

Pop is listening to the radio.

live

Rob lives on an island. His home is there.

long

The snake is long. It is not short.

look

Fifi is looking at a picture.

look for

Henry is looking for a book. He is trying to find it.

lorry

Henry is driving a lorry.

lost

Henry is lost. He does not know where he is.

lot

There are a lot of birds in the tree.

loud

The band plays loud music. It is very noisy.

love

Sam loves Fifi.

low

The wall is low. It is not high.

lunch

Zizi eats lunch at midday.

M m

machine

All these machines work.

magazine

Henry is reading a magazine.

magician

This is a magician. A magician does tricks.

make

Ben is making a cake.

man

One man and two women.

many

The man has many magazines for sale.

map

Henry is looking at a map to see where to go.

mark

There is a mark on the map.

market

This is a market in the street.

marry

Sam is marrying Fifi.

mask

Who is wearing the mask?

match

Fred lights a match.

measure

Fifi measures Zizi to find out how tall she is.

meat

The butcher sells meat.

medicine

The nurse is giving Zizi medicine to make her better.

meet

Bill and Ben meet.

melt

The ice cream is melting.

mend

Ben is mending his bicycle.

menu

Fifi reads the menu to choose what to eat.

45

metal

Cars are made of metal.

middle

The pig is in the middle.

milk

Zizi is drinking milk.

minute

There are 60 seconds in a minute.

There are 60 minutes in an hour.

mirror

The cat is looking at himself in the mirror.

miss

Henry misses the bus.

model

Fritz is making a model aeroplane.

money

Ben is counting his money.

monkey

The monkey is swinging from a tree.

monster

The monster is friendly.

month

There are twelve months in the year: January, February, March, April, May, June, July, August, September, October, November and December.

moon

The moon shines in the sky at night.

more

Bill has more money than Ben.

morning

Morning is the part of day before midday.

We get up in the morning.

People go to work and school in the morning.

most

Most of the apples are red. Nearly all of them are red.

mother

Mary is Zizi's mother. Zizi is her daughter.

motorbike

Henry is riding a motorbike.

mountain

This is a high mountain.

mouse, mice

One mouse is pink. The other mice are grey.

moustache

This man has a very long moustache.

mouth

He has a big mouth.

move

Bill and Ben are moving the table.

much

Have you much money? Have you a lot of money?

I feel much better today. I feel a lot better.

You are making too much noise.

mud

The monster is playing in the mud.

mushroom

The mouse is dancing on the mushroom.

music

The band is playing music.

Nn

nail

Henry is hitting a nail with his hammer.

name

Zizi has written her name.

naughty

Zizi is being naughty. She is not being good.

near

The tree is near the house. It is close to the house.

neck

A giraffe has a long neck.

necklace

Fifi is wearing a necklace.

need

Zizi needs a bath because she is dirty.

needle

Fifi is threading a needle.

nest

The baby birds are in a nest.

never

Fifi never eats cheese. She does not eat any cheese at any time.

I never watch television.

Pop never goes out.

new

Ben has a new car. It is not old.

newspaper

Bill is reading a newspaper.

next

Fifi is sitting next to Sam.

night

It is night, not day.

nobody

Nobody is wearing a hat.

noise

Zizi is making a noise.

north

The bird is facing North. North is opposite South.

nose

Henry's nose is red.

notebook

The man is looking at his notebook.

nothing

There is nothing in the box. It is empty.

notice

Fred is reading a notice.

now

Come here now, not later! Come here this minute!

Fifi was here this morning but she is not here now.

He must be at home by now.

number

These are all numbers.

nurse

The nurse is giving Ben some medicine because he is ill.

nut

Zizi is eating a nut.

octopus

The octopus lives in the sea.

offer

Sam offers Fifi flowers. He is giving them to her.

office

Jake works in an office.

often

The telephone often rings. It rings many times a day.

oil

Tim puts oil on his bicycle. He is oiling it.

old

Pop is an old man. He is not young.

on

The cup is on the table.

onion

Henry is slicing an onion.

only

Only one pig is black.

open

Fifi opens the door to the postman.

open

The shop is open. People can go into it.

opposite

Ben is sitting opposite Bill.

or

Which shoes do you want? The blue ones or the red ones?

You must choose one of the two pairs.

You can either sit here or there.

Shall we walk or cycle?

orange

Henry's socks are orange.

orange

An orange is orange.

order

Fritz orders dinner. He tells the waiter what to bring.

other

Where is Henry's other sock?

out

The toys are out of the box. They are not in it.

outside

Zizi is playing outside. She is not inside.

over

The pig is jumping over the fence.

owl

The owl is sitting in the tree.

page

On the first page of the book is a picture of a mouse.

paint

The artist is painting a picture.

paints

These are her paints.

pair

A pair of orange socks.

palace

The king lives in a palace.

pancake

Bill is tossing a pancake.

paper

Zizi is painting a picture on a piece of paper.

parachute

The parachute is coming down.

parcel

The postman has brought a parcel for Aggie.

parents

Zizi's mother and father are her parents.

park

Fifi is walking in the park.

park

Henry is parking his car.

parrot

The parrot is laughing.

party

Fifi is having a party.

pass

Henry passes Bruno. He goes past him.

passport

Ben shows his passport. He is going to another country.

path

The path goes across the field.

patient

The patient is in bed. He is in hospital.

pavement

Fifi is standing on the pavement.

paw

The cat is licking its paw.

pay

Fifi pays for the bread. She gives Ben money for it.

peach

Bill is eating a peach.

pear

Ben is eating a pear.

pea

Zizi is eating peas.

pen

Fifi writes with a pen.

pencil

She draws with a pencil.

people

These people are talking.

pepper

Ben puts pepper on his food.

perhaps

Perhaps it will rain. It may rain, but it is not certain.

Perhaps he is lost. He might be lost.

Perhaps I shall go tomorrow, but I am not sure.

petrol

Henry puts petrol in his car to make it go.

photograph

This is a photograph of Fifi.

piano

Fritz plays the piano.

pick

The people are picking pears.

pick up

Fifi picks up a pear she has dropped.

picnic

Bill, Ben and Fifi are having a picnic.

picture

This is a picture of the picnic.

pie

Bill is cutting the pie.

piece

Zizi is eating a piece of the pie.

pig

The pig is pink.

pile

Henry is carrying a pile of books.

pillow

Zizi's pillow is blue.

pilot

A pilot flies an aeroplane.

pin

Bill pricks Ben with a pin.

pinch

Bill pinches Ben.

pineapple

A big pineapple.

pink

The big pig is pink.

pipe

Ben is smoking a pipe.

place

Ben is looking for a place to have a picnic. He is looking for somewhere to have it.

Where is my place? Where am I sitting?

Here is an empty place.

plant

Henry has a big plant.

plant

He is planting it in the garden.

plate

The chips are on a plate.

play

The children are playing.

pocket

There is a handkerchief in the pocket.

point

Ben is pointing at Bill.

policeman

The policeman is pointing at Bill.

polish

Fritz is polishing the table to make it shine.

polite

Bill is very polite. He is not rude.

It is polite to say "please" when you ask for something.

pond

The ducks are swimming on a pond.

pony

Henry is riding a pony. A pony is a small horse.

poor

This man is poor. He has not much money.

pork

Fritz is eating pork. Pork is meat from a pig.

port

The ship is in the port.

porter

A porter carries suitcases.

postcard

Fifi is writing a postcard.

postman

The postman brings letters.

post office

Fifi is at the post office. She is buying stamps.

potato

Henry is peeling a potato.

pour

Henry is pouring wine on to the table.

pram

Fifi is in her pram.

present

Henry gives Fifi a present.

pretend

Fifi is pretending to be a ghost. She acts like one.

pretty

Fifi is a pretty girl.

price

What price are the potatoes? How much do they cost?

prize

Henry has won a prize for coming first.

promise

Fifi promises to send Henry a postcard.
She says she will definitely send him one.

Dad has promised to take us to the zoo tomorrow.

pudding

Zizi likes pudding because it is sweet.

pull

Bill and Ben are both pulling the rope

puppet

The puppet is dancing.

puppy

A puppy is a baby dog.

purple

The king has a purple coat.

purse

Fifi puts money in her purse.

push

Bill is pushing Ben.

put

Fifi puts milk in the fridge.

puzzle

Fritz is doing a puzzle.

pyjamas

Henry is wearing pyjamas. He wears them in bed.

queen

The queen wears a crown.

question

The queen asks the king a question. She asks him something and wants him to give her an answer.

Please answer my question!

The question has no answer.

queue

Henry is standing in a queue.

quiet

The burglar is very quiet. He does not make any noise.

quite

The film is quite good but the book is better.

He is quite clever. He could be more clever.

I quite like him, but I do not like him very much.

rabbit

The rabbit is running.

race

The rabbits are having a race. Which one will win?

radiator

The cat is asleep under the radiator. It is warm there.

radio

Pop is listening to the radio.

railway line

The rabbit is sitting on the railway line.

rain

It is raining.

rainbow

There is a rainbow in the sky.

raincoat

Henry is wearing a raincoat to keep him dry.

raspberry

A dish of raspberries.

rat

The rat is chasing a rabbit.

razor

Sam shaves with a razor.

reach

Fifi cannot reach the book. It is too high.

read

Fifi is reading the book.

real

This is a real elephant. It is not a pretend one.

receive

Fifi receives a letter. The postman gives it to her.

recognise

Fritz recognises Fifi. He knows her because he has met her before.

Do you recognise me? Can you remember who I am?

I recognise that writing. It is Fifi's writing.

record

Bill puts on a record to hear some music.

red

Fifi is painting the chair red.

refuse

The donkey refuses to move. He will not move.

remember

Fritz remembers Fifi. He has not forgotten her.

Henry cannot remember where he put his book. He has forgotten where he put it.

Can you remember your holiday last year?

rest

Henry is resting because he is tired.

ribbon

Zizi is wearing a blue ribbon in her hair.

rice

Wong Fu is eating rice.

rich

This man is rich. He has a lot of money.

ride

Henry is riding a donkey.

right

Fifi raises her right hand.

ring

The thief is wearing a ring.

ring

The telephone is ringing.

river

The river is wide. It is a long way across.

road

There are sheep on the road.

roar

The lion is roaring. He is making a noise.

rock

Henry is sitting on a rock in the sea.

roof

The house has a red roof.

room

This is a room in a house.

root

The plant has long roots. They grow under the ground.

rope

Henry is up a rope.

rose

Fifi is smelling a rose.

rough

The road is rough. It is not smooth.

round

The table is round.

row

A row of flowers.

row

Bill is rowing a boat.

rub

The cat is rubbing its back.

run

Henry is running away.

sack

The thief is carrying a sack.

sad

Henry is sad.
He is not happy.

safe

Henry is safe. He is not in danger.

sail

Fifi is sailing a boat.

sailor

The sailor is in his boat.

salad

This is a mixed salad. It is made of vegetables.

salt

Bill puts salt on the salad.

same

The girls are wearing the same hat.

sand

Zizi is digging in the sand.

sandal

A pair of sandals.

sandwich

The mouse is eating a big sandwich.

satchel

Tim has a red satchel.

sauce

Fifi is pouring sauce over the ice cream.

saucepan

Ben picks up the saucepan.

saucer

The cup is on a saucer.

sausage

Ben is eating sausages.

saw

Bill is sawing wood with a saw.

say

Pop does not say much. He does not talk much.

Bill says he is rich. He tells us he is rich.

The letter says they are well.

scales

Fifi stands on the scales to weigh herself.

scarf

Henry has a very long scarf round his neck.

school

The children are at school.

scissors

Fifi is cutting the hair with a pair of scissors.

scratch

Ruff is scratching his ear.

sea

The sea is blue.

seal

The seal is in the sea.

see

Zizi can see the seal. She is looking at it.

seed

Dan is planting seeds. They will grow into plants.

seem

Dan seems to be angry. He looks as if he is angry.

sell

The baker is selling some bread to Fifi.

send

Fifi is sending a letter. She is posting it.

sentence

This is a sentence. It has four words in it.

serve

The waiter is serving Fifi. He is giving her food.

sew

Henry is sewing.

sewing machine

Henry is using a sewing machine.

shadow

Zizi is looking at her shadow on the ground.

shake

Bill is shaking the tree.

shape

These are different shapes.

share

Bill and Ben share the cake. They each have a piece.

shark

The shark is chasing Henry.

sharp

The knife is sharp. It cuts well.

sheep

The three sheep are standing in a row.

sheet

Fifi puts a sheet on the bed.

shell

Zizi is holding a shell. She found it on the beach.

ship

The ship is at sea.

shirt

Fritz has a blue shirt.

shoe

The shoes are red.

shop

Fifi is going into a shop to buy things.

short

The yellow snake is short. The red snake is long.

shorts

Henry is wearing a pair of white shorts.

shoulder

The bird is sitting on the man's shoulder.

shout

Ben is shouting at Bill.

show

Fifi shows Pop her picture.

shower

Henry is having a shower.

shut

The gate is shut. It is not open.

side

One side of the box is pink.

silver

Fifi has a silver bracelet.

since

Fifi has not seen Ben since Tuesday. Tuesday was the last time she saw him.

Since it is sunny, I will go for a walk. I will go because it is sunny.

sing

The people are singing.

sister

Zizi and Daisy are sisters.

sit

Zizi is sitting on a chair.

sitting room

This is a sitting room.

skate

Fifi and Henry are skating.

ski

Henry is putting on his skis.

ski

Henry is skiing.

skin

An elephant has grey skin.

skirt

Fifi is wearing a red skirt.

sky

The bird is in the sky. The sky is blue.

sleep

Zizi is sleeping. She is not awake.

sleeve

The shirt only has one sleeve.

slice

Bill is cutting a slice of bread.

slide

Henry is sliding along the ice on his bottom.

slide

This is a slide. It is a kind of photograph.

slipper

Zizi's slippers are red. She wears them at home.

slowly

A snail moves slowly.

small

The brown bear is small.

smell

Fifi smells the perfume. It smells nice.

smile

Fifi is smiling. She is happy.

smoke

Pop is smoking a pipe.

snail

Here is the snail again.

snake

The snake is in the grass.

snow

It is snowing. Zizi is playing in the snow.

soap

Ben has soap on his face.

sock

Zizi is wearing pink socks.

sofa

Fifi is sitting on a sofa.

soft

The cushion is soft. It is not hard.

soldier

The soldier is in the army.

some

Some of the soldiers are smiling and some are not.

someone
Someone has stolen my car.

something
There is something in my eye.

sometimes
Sometimes I am sad.

son

Henry is Pop's son.
Pop is Henry's father.

song

The singer is singing a song.

soon

We will go home soon. We will go in a short time from now.

I want to go as soon as possible.

Soon we are going on holiday.

sort

The men are wearing three different sorts of hat.

soup

Henry is eating soup.

south

The bird is facing south. South is opposite north.

space

The astronaut is floating in space.

spade

Dan is digging with a spade.

speak

Fifi is speaking to Pop. She is talking to him.

spell

Zizi can spell her name. She knows how to write it.

spend

Ben is spending money. He is paying for things.

spider

The spider frightens Fifi.

spoon

Zizi is eating with a spoon.

spot

Zizi has lots of spots.

spread

Bill is spreading butter on the bread.

square

This is a square. A square is a shape.

stable

The horse lives in a stable.

stairs

Zizi is going up the stairs.

stamp

There are two stamps on the envelope.

stand

Bill is standing on Ben's back.

star

The star shines in the sky at night.

start

This is the start of the race. It is about to begin.

station

The train is in the station.

statue

Henry is looking at a statue.

stay

Stay here. Do not go away.

Fifi is staying in bed. She is not getting up.

Henry is staying in Paris for four days. He will spend four days there.

steal

Fred is stealing jewellery. He is a thief.

stem

The caterpillar is on the stem of the flower.

steps

The cat is sitting on the steps.

stereo

Ben turns on the stereo.

stick

Dan is carrying sticks.

stocking

Fifi is wearing a pair of black stockings.

stone

Zizi picks up a stone on the beach.

stop

The car stops at the traffic lights.

storm

This is a storm. The weather is very bad.

story

Pop is reading the children an exciting story.

straight

The road is very straight. It does not bend.

strawberry

Zizi is eating a strawberry.

stream

Fifi is crossing a stream.

street

This is a street in a town.

string

The mouse is taking away a piece of the string.

striped

Fifi has a striped dress.

strong

Sam is strong. He is not weak.

stupid

Henry is feeling stupid. He does not feel clever.

submarine

The submarine is underwater.

suddenly

The car stops suddenly. It stops very quickly.

sugar

Fifi is putting sugar in her tea.

suit

Henry is wearing a suit.

suitcase

Ben is carrying a suitcase.
He is going on holiday.

sun

The sun is shining. It is a sunny day.

supermarket

Fifi is at the supermarket. She is shopping.

surprise

Fifi has a surprise. She did not expect a party.

surround

The birds have surrounded the cat.

swallow

The snake has swallowed a ball. He has eaten it.

swan

The swan is swimming.

sweet

Zizi is eating sweets.

swim

Bill and Ben are swimming.

swimsuit

Fifi has a striped swimsuit.

swimming pool

The man is diving into the swimming pool.

swing

Ben is swinging on a swing.

table

The cat is sitting on the table.

tail

One cat has a tail. The other one has not.

tall

The woman is tall. The man is small.

take

Zizi is taking a chocolate.

tap

The tap is running. The mouse has turned it on.

taste

Ben is tasting the sauce to see what it is like.

taxi

Fritz calls a taxi.

tea

Fifi has a cup of tea.

teacher

The teacher is with his class. He is teaching them.

team

This is a football team.

teapot

Fifi is pouring the tea from the teapot.

tear

Henry tears his trousers.

tear

Zizi has tears on her face. She has been crying.

teddy bear

Zizi has a teddy bear.

teeth

The rat has sharp teeth.

telephone

The telephone is ringing.

television

The children are watching television.

tell

Pop is telling the children an exciting story.

tennis

The men are playing tennis.

tent

Henry is looking out of the tent.

thank

Fifi thanks Ben for the present he has given her.

that

That is my car.

I want that apple there, not this one here.

That bicycle belongs to me. It is mine.

theatre

Fifi is at the theatre. She is watching a play.

then

He ate his dinner, then he had a piece of cake. After his dinner he had a piece of cake.

We did not have a car then. We did not have one at that time.

there

The car is not there. It is not in that place.

Where did you put your bag? Did you put it here or there?

There is a theatre in the town.

thick

The slice of bread is thick. It is not thin.

thief

The thief is stealing jewels.

thin

The man is thin. The woman is fat.

thing

There are ten things on the tray. What are they?

think

Fifi is thinking about Sam.

thirsty

The man is thirsty. He wants something to drink.

this

Take this hat (the one here) not that hat (the one there).

This dress is pretty but that one is not.

This is an elephant and that is a camel.

through

The king is coming through the door.

throw

Zizi is throwing bread to the ducks.

thumb

Henry hits his thumb.

ticket

Fifi shows the conductor her ticket.

tie

Henry has a spotted tie.

tie

Bill is tying a knot in the string.

tiger

The tiger is roaring.

tights

The red tights are hanging on the line.

tired

Henry is tired. He has been running.

to

The children go to school.

Fifi is going to work.

Henry is going to the station to catch a train.

Bill gives an apple to Ben.

today

It is Zizi's birthday today. It is on this day.

toe

The mouse is tickling someone's toes.

together

The cats sleep together. They sleep with each other.

tomato

Henry is slicing a tomato.

tomorrow

Tomorrow is the day after today.

Today is Monday so tomorrow will be Tuesday.

The day after tomorrow is Wednesday.

tongue

Ruff has a pink tongue.

too

The coat is too small. It is not big enough.

tool

The tools are in a box.

toothbrush

The mouse is holding a yellow toothbrush.

toothpaste

There is toothpaste on the toothbrush.

top

Ben is at the top of the stepladder.

touch

The policeman touches the thief on the shoulder.

towards

The cat is walking towards the milk.

towel

Henry is drying himself with a yellow towel.

tower

This is a famous tower. Where is it?

town

This is a town. There are many houses in it.

toy

Zizi is playing with a toy.

tractor

Henry is driving a tractor.

traffic lights

Henry hits the traffic lights.

73

train

Henry gets on a train.

treasure

Ali has found some treasure.

tree

The giraffe is eating the green leaves on the tree.

triangle

These are all triangles. A triangle is a shape.

trousers

Ben is wearing red trousers.

trumpet

Ben is playing a trumpet.

tulip

The tulips are in a vase.

turn

The car is turning left.

type

Henry is typing.

typewriter

His typewriter is broken.

tyre

The bicycle has two flat tyres.

twin

Bella and Betty are twins.

ugly

The monster is ugly. He is not beautiful.

umbrella

Henry's umbrella blows away.

uncle

Tom is Zizi's uncle. He is Aunt Aggie's husband.

under

The cat is under the bed.

underground

An underground station.

understand

I understand what he says. I know what he means.

I understand how this machine works. I know how it works.

I can understand French.

undress

Fifi is undressing Zizi. She is taking off her clothes.

unhappy

Henry is unhappy. He is not happy.

until

Ben is not coming home until Wednesday. He will not come home before then.

Wait until I come back.

We cannot go away until tomorrow.

up

Henry is going up a ladder. He is not going down it.

upstairs

The cat is upstairs. It is not downstairs.

use

Fifi is using a knife to cut the bread.

useful

The knife is useful. It helps her to cut things.

vacuum cleaner

The vacuum cleaner cleans the carpet.

valley

There is a river in the valley.

van

Henry is driving a van.

vase

The vase is full of flowers.

vegetable

These are all vegetables.

very

Ben speaks French well. Henry speaks French very well. He speaks it even better than Ben.

A mouse is small. An insect is smaller. It is very small.

village

A village is smaller than a town.

violin

Henry plays the violin.

visit

Fifi is visiting Pop. She has come to see him.

voice

Pop has a quiet voice. He speaks quietly.

Ben has a low voice and Fifi has a high voice.

When you shout, your voice gets louder.

wait

Aggie is waiting for a bus.

waiter

The waiter is serving Fifi.

wake

Henry is waking up. It is morning.

wall

The cats are sitting on top of the wall.

wallpaper

Bill is putting up wallpaper.

walk

Fifi is going for a walk.

want

Zizi wants a cake. She hopes she can have one.

war

Two countries are at war when they fight each other.

The war has lasted ten years.

wardrobe

Fifi looks in the wardrobe. She hangs clothes there.

warm

Fifi is warm. She is lying in the sun.

wash

Henry is washing his face to make it clean.

wash basin

The frog is jumping out of the wash basin.

washing machine

The washing machine is on. It is washing clothes.

wasp

The wasp has stung Henry.

watch

Fifi looks at her watch to see what time it is.

water

The water is running out of the bath.

waterfall

Tarzan is crossing the waterfall.

wave

Ben dives under the wave.

weak

Henry is weak. He is not strong.

wear

Fifi is wearing a hat.

wedding

A wedding at the church.

weigh

Fifi is weighing the flour.

west

The bird is facing west. West is opposite east.

wet

The dog is very wet. He is not dry.

wheel

The bicycle has one big wheel and one small wheel.

wheelbarrow

The wheelbarrow is full.

when

When does the last train go? At what time does it go?

I had a car when I lived in Paris. I had a car then.

Come when you have finished. Come after you have finished.

where

Where is the cat? Can you see it?

which

Which cat is the biggest? Which cat is the smallest?

while

Zizi is dreaming while she sleeps.

whisper

Fifi is whispering to Ben. She is talking quietly.

whistle

The man is blowing a whistle.

white

The fat cat is white. The thin cat is black.

who

Who is wearing a hat? Which person?

why

Why is Henry up a tree? For what reason?

wide

The river is very wide. It is not narrow.

wife

Heidi is Fritz's wife. He is her husband.

win

Sam wins the race. He has come first.

wind

The wind is blowing.

window

The thief breaks the window.

windmill

This is a windmill.

wine

Henry pours a glass of wine.

wing

The bird is flapping its wings.

wipe

Bill is wiping the table.

wire

The fence is made of wire.

witch

The witch is flying.

with

The witch with her cat on the broom.

without

The witch without her cat on the broom.

wood

The table is made of wood. Wood comes from trees.

wool

Three balls of wool.

woman

Fifi is a woman. Henry is a man.

word

Zizi is writing a word.

work

Ben is working hard.

world

This is a map of the world.

worm

The bird looks at the worm.

wrap

Fifi is wrapping a present.

write

Fifi is writing a letter.

wrong

The answer is wrong. It is not right.

yacht

The yacht is at sea.

year

There are 365 days in a year.

There are 12 months or 52 weeks in a year.

There are 100 years in a century.

yellow

The chick is yellow.

yesterday

Yesterday was the day before today.

Today is Monday, yesterday was Sunday.

young

A puppy is a young dog. It is not an old dog.

zebra

A zebra has a striped coat.

zoo

Zizi sees animals at the zoo. The zebra is there.

Parts of speech

There are several different kinds of words. Some words name things, some are "doing" words and some join different parts of a sentence together. There are eight main types of word and they are usually called "parts of speech". It is a good idea to understand what each type of word does, as it will help you to speak and write good English. It will also help you when you learn a foreign language.

noun	This a word used for naming a person, animal, place or thing.	e.g. Fifi, mouse, Africa, book The <u>book</u> is on the <u>table</u>.
pronoun	A pronoun is a word which takes the place of a noun. It refers to a person, animal, place or thing without giving its name.	e.g. I, you, he, she, it, they, who, what, which <u>It</u> is on the table.
adjective	This is a word used to describe a noun or a pronoun.	e.g. big, small, dangerous, new, wooden The book is <u>big</u>.
verb	This is a "doing" or "action" word. It tells you what someone or something is doing.	e.g. run, sleep, catch, eat Henry <u>is running</u>.
adverb	This is a word which describes or tells you more about a verb, an adjective or an adverb.	e.g. quickly, soon, very, rather Henry is running <u>fast</u>. The man is <u>very</u> tall.
preposition	A preposition tells you where people or things are in relation to each other.	e.g. with, under, on, in The cat is <u>under</u> the table.
conjunction	This is a link word which is used to join words or groups of words.	e.g. and, but, when, then Here are Bill <u>and</u> Ben. Zizi had her tea <u>then</u> went to bed.
interjection	This is an exclamation. It is usually a short word.	e.g. Oh! Hello! "<u>Oops</u>!" said Henry.

Useful words

Numbers

1	one	21	twenty-one
2	two	22	twenty-two
3	three	23	twenty-three
4	four	24	twenty-four
5	five	25	twenty-five
6	six	26	twenty-six
7	seven	27	twenty-seven
8	eight	28	twenty-eight
9	nine	29	twenty-nine
10	ten	30	thirty
11	eleven	40	forty
12	twelve	50	fifty
13	thirteen	60	sixty
14	fourteen	70	seventy
15	fifteen	80	eighty
16	sixteen	90	ninety
17	seventeen	100	one hundred
18	eighteen	1,000,000	one million
19	nineteen		
20	twenty		

1st	first	7th	seventh
2nd	second	8th	eighth
3rd	third	9th	ninth
4th	fourth	10th	tenth
5th	fifth	20th	twentieth
6th	sixth	50th	fiftieth

The days of the week

Monday
Tuesday
Wednesday
Thursday
Friday
Saturday
Sunday

The months of the year

January
February
March
April
May
June
July
August
September
October
November
December

The seasons

Spring
Summer
Autumn
Winter

Countries and continents

Africa	Denmark	Ireland	Soviet Union
Asia	England	Italy	Spain
Australia	Europe	Japan	Switzerland
Austria	France	The Netherlands	United States
Belgium	Germany	New Zealand	Wales
Canada	Great Britain	Poland	Yugoslavia
China	Hungary	Scotland	
Czechoslovakia	India	South America	